First published in the United States in 1999 by Peter Bedrick Books
A division of NTC/Contemporary Publishing Group, Inc
4255 West Touhy Avenue
Lincolnwood (Chicago), Illinois 60646-1975 U.S.A.

Editor: Lisa Edwards
Designer: Celia Hart
Natural History Consultant: Cherry Alexander

Library of Congress Cataloging-in-Publication Data is available from the
United States Library of Congress.

Printed and bound in Portugal by Edições ASA

International Standard Book Number: 0-87226-540-4

00 01 02 03 04 05 15 14 13 12 11 10 9 8 7 6 5 4 3 2 1

2070772

LOOK WHO LIVES IN...

The Arctic

ALAN BAKER

PETER BEDRICK BOOKS
NEW YORK

As winter turns into spring in the cold, cold Arctic, something is looking at a mosquito. It's a fluttering, flitting...

butterfly!
It has golden-brown wings and
     a furry body. Gazing from a
grey, granite rock, something
is looking at the butterfly.
It's a lively little…

lemming!
It has black, beady eyes
and a short, stubby tail.
Sitting amongst the Arctic flowers,
something is looking at the lemming.
It's an alert, agile...

Arctic hare!
It has long, pointed ears.
Watching from the windy wasteland,
something is looking at the
Arctic hare.
It's a swift, sprightly…

Arctic fox!
It has a thick, white coat for warmth.
Floating through the freezing air,
something is looking at the Arctic fox.
It's a silently swooping…

snowy owl!
It has bright, yellow eyes and long,
sharp talons. Moving stealthily
across a frosted plain,
something is looking
at the snowy owl.
It's a growling, prowling...

grey wolf!
It has long, lean legs
and sharp, pointed teeth.
High up on an icy ledge, something
is looking at the grey wolf.
It's a restless, roaming…

reindeer!
It has beautiful, branched antlers
and broad, flat hooves.
Flopping on the floating ice,
something is looking at the reindeer.
It's a silky, slippery…

21

seal!
It has a long, sleek body
and powerful flippers.
Breathing in the freezing air,
something is looking at the seal.
It's a weary, waddling…

walrus!
It has long, thick whiskers,
just like a moustache!
Peering from a floating iceberg,
something is looking at the walrus.
 It's a powerful, prowling…

polar bear!
The polar bear can
see all the animals:
the mosquito, the
butterfly, the lemming,

the Arctic hare, the Arctic fox, the snowy owl, the grey wolf, the reindeer, the seal and the walrus.
Can *you* see them?

The World's Arctic Region

The map below shows the Arctic Circle — the most northern part of the Earth. The center of the Circle is called the North Pole. The Arctic Ocean takes up most of this area, and part of it is always frozen. The rest is made up of parts of the countries shown below. In some areas during the Arctic winter, the sun may not be seen for over two months. But in summer, the sun may never set.

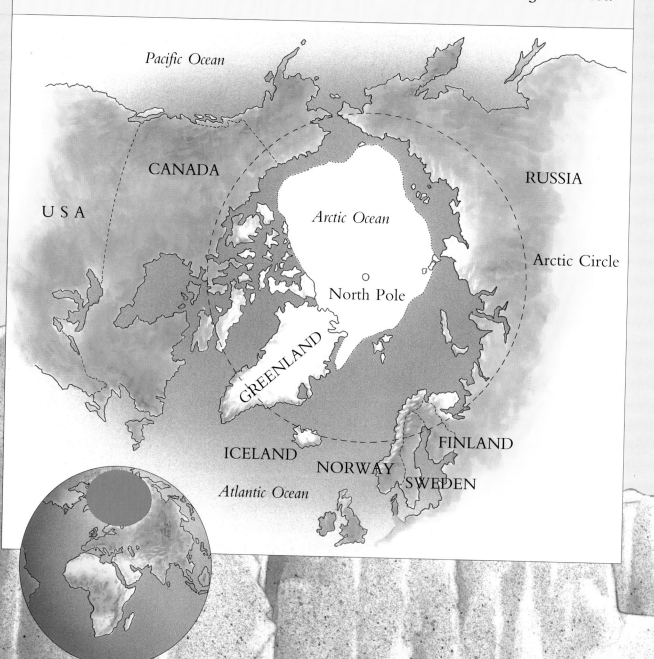

Pacific Ocean

CANADA

RUSSIA

USA

Arctic Ocean

Arctic Circle

○ North Pole

GREENLAND

ICELAND

FINLAND

NORWAY

SWEDEN

Atlantic Ocean

Index

 Arctic fox, page 15: Arctic foxes can often be seen eating the remains of polar bears' meals. Their fur changes from white in winter to bluish-grey in summer.

 Arctic hare, page 13: The Arctic hare is greyish-brown in the summer, but turns white in the winter. It has hair under its feet to keep it from slipping in the snow.

 Butterfly, page 8: Like many other Arctic butterflies the Polaris Fritillary takes two years to change from a caterpillar into a butterfly.

 Grey wolf, page 18: Grey wolves live in large packs and will eat most small animals and birds. They will attack large animals when they are very hungry.

 Lemming, page 10: Lemmings live in grass nests, in tunnels that they dig under the snow. They breed quickly and move around in large numbers to find food.

 Mosquito, page 7: Mosquitoes can be found in large numbers in the Arctic during spring and summer. They pierce the skin of animals and suck their blood.

 Polar bear, page 26: Male polar bears can grow up to 9 feet tall and weigh almost a ton. They feed mainly on walruses and seals.

 Reindeer, page 21: Reindeer are protected from the cold by two coats of thick hair. The outer coat changes from dark brown in summer to light brown in winter.

 Seal, page 22: Ringed seals are excellent swimmers and grow to about 5 feet in length. Females give birth to their young in ice dens under the snow.

 Snowy owl, page 17: The snowy owl has a wing span of up to 5 feet. Most owls hunt at night, but the snowy owl hunts in the daytime.

 Walrus, page 24: Walruses measure more than 10 feet in length and can weigh up to 3,000 pounds. They use their tusks to pick out small creatures from the sea bed.

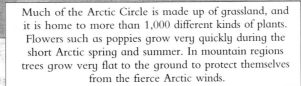 Much of the Arctic Circle is made up of grassland, and it is home to more than 1,000 different kinds of plants. Flowers such as poppies grow very quickly during the short Arctic spring and summer. In mountain regions trees grow very flat to the ground to protect themselves from the fierce Arctic winds.